Works and Days

PITT POETRY SERIES

Ed Ochester, Editor

Works and Days

Edward Kleinschmidt Mayes

Edward Mayes

to Alvin —
all thanks &

UNIVERSITY OF PITTSBURGH PRESS

amore.

Ed
November 1999

Published by the University of Pittsburgh Press, Pittsburgh, Pa., 15261
Copyright © 1999, Edward Kleinschmidt Mayes
All rights reserved
Manufactured in the United States of America
Printed on acid-free paper
10 9 8 7 6 5 4 3 2 1

This book is the winner of the 1998 Associated Writing Programs' Award Series in Poetry. Associated Writing Programs, a national organization serving over 150 colleges and universities, has its headquarters at George Mason University, Tallwood House, Mail Stop 1E3, Fairfax, Va. 23030.

A CIP catalog record for this book is available from the Library of Congress and the British Library.

For Frances, *sempre*.

Contents

Ago 1

Buii 4

Campo 6

Dove 8

Erbaccia 11

Fabbro 14

Giorni 16

Io 19

Lavoro 22

Macchina 24

Notizia 27

Oliveto 31

Porca Miseria 34

Qua 37

Raccolta 40

Sfuso 43

Terreno 46

Uva 49

Verità 52

Zappa 56

Acknowledgments 61

Works and Days

A*go*

Amo
amas

amat: thus—that which I've tattooed on my heart.
I found yesterday the short black pieces of thread

that were stitches, could have come from the balls
of a matador gored by a bull, or those pulled out

with tweezers not long after the vasectomy. We've seen
the old photo of the prizefighter, his right eye

stitched shut, puffed up. My uncle was the one
to heat the needle hot, slide it into my infected thumb

and the creamy pus ran out as I shouted. After me,
you. After me, dear reader, you. *Mi dica*, they ask me

---

ago: needle
amo, amas, amat: I love, you love, he, she, it loves
mi dica: tell me

at Molesini's. And I answer, *Ricotta*—it's recooked.
Drizzle chestnut honey on it they tell me. So much

sounds so good that I can taste the sound. After my mother
moved her Singer from the farm to town, she electrified it.

Everything seemed hemmed then by noon. There was time then,
attics stuffed with poems. In March, the Ides, in fact, Zappini

gave me a lesson in chain saws, and I cut through the dead
of a hundreds-of-years-old olive in order to save

that which was wanting to be alive, and it felt
like cutting through someone's elbow, someone I knew,

in order to allow the hand to relax, to unfist itself, and both
branch and arm, still communicating to all parts, across space

that wasn't there before. I'm telling you this because I still like
to count to five on each hand, fingers unlike needles, jointed and

pointing in other directions than north. Shall I string these grapevines
in trees, as the Etruscans who lived and died here did? We who try

to understand what sorrow has fastened so. The cold needle floats
on the still water. There are those times when the water in our own lives

needs to be reboiled in order for it to be drunk again. Close the shutters we seem to always have open and let in a fine steel needle of light—

what other time, if not now, for some kinds of darknesses, i buii.

---

i buii: the darknesses

Buii

Bugie—good word, as in *le bugie hanno le gambe corte*,
but then does truth wear long beautiful trousers?
A little light, please. Donatella says, "It's a small
world of thieves," "a world of small thieves."

Where is the soul, you might ask, in all this dark rubble?
Bivio: Bettarelli braids twenty-six onions—they hang in deep
kitchen darkness. They came from as much earth as I will go
into. And the lemon trees we have out back are in pots

and so the winter won't kill them we bring them
into the *limonaia*—lemons too tart, too sweet,
come si dice. The squeeze of them, like squeezing souls,
bright yellow ones, and the juice of souls! Bivio:

Chiuso per lutto I see on the shop and think the mother has
finally died and they're in their dark clothes, the wool ones they

---

le bugie hanno le gambe corte: lies have short legs
bivio: detour, fork in the road, dilemma
limonaia: place for storing lemon trees in the winter
come si dice: how does one say
chiuso per lutto: closed for mourning

keep hidden in a chest. Dethrone the prince of darkness, his
likeness floating in a bowl of blood. Vessel of wind smashed,

shards shoved in cracks of walls to keep the wind out. Bivio:
acqua in bocca—can you keep secrets? The road here is lined
with hedges, boxwood and laurel, slow and small-leaved, fast
and large-leaved. We shear both, steel blades swishing, cutting

green air, and feel cut by what we've cut but not hurt, like the plums
are when they fall and roll under our feet, but cut by what we cut,
what we cut living longer than those of us who do the cutting.
The obscure can be the best narcotic. The obvious has no *bivio* to it.

Bivio: men and women working in the fields—you've seen pictures—
roots have no place else to go but into darkness. And here's Giorgio
on his blue Pasquali, three plowshares riding behind, willing to turn
up, turn over the dark earth of the *campo*.

---

acqua in bocca: literally, "water in the mouth," to hold a secret
campo: field

Campo

Can anyone tell me where the closest field of vision is? Here I am,
an American of Polish descent, my head full of Tuscan *campi* cut
into the side of Monte S. Egidio, recalling the English writer Langland's
Piers Plowman turning topsoil to try to explain something so clear that
it needs no explaining. Forgive the rattling, unless you like it—the sound
the *ceci* make inside their tan husks. Zappini pulls them up and dries them
in the crotches of olives and in August rubs them between his hands
for *brodo* that evening. Forgive any *campanilismo*, but when I hear the church
bells at Torreone do their *Angelus*, I do stop working and scan the skies, and
think back thirty years ago, third-graders on the playgrounds of St.
    Stanislaus,
doing the same. Ann says I'm playing Daphnis, Sicilian shepherd and
    poet,
and yes, but also Cain, especially in March, when I'm burning *erbaccia*,
and the wind shifts toward me and I walk out of clouds of smoke, not
changed into someone or something else, or not as if I've seen plumes of
Giove, just me coughing, lungs full of the final end of *erbacce*. But do

---

ceci: chick-peas
brodo: broth
campanilismo: parochialism; dedication to the bell tower of one's village
erbaccia: weeds
Giove: Jupiter

weeds have a final end? Ask any gardener, ask anyone who is serious
    about
wandering through the garden. Dante took his fields with him his
    twenty years
of exile, to Verona, to Ravenna, and Boccaccio took them back to Firenze
fifty years later when he read the *Commedia* aloud to that city. I know
that the field of vision is spiritual earth. I hope to have enough life
to work the narrow terraces by hand, those Giorgio's Pasquali can't reach.
I think of the souls of the two young Cortona boys the retreating
Germans killed in early June 1944, there on the third *campo*, while
gathering strawberries in baskets their fathers made. They are an offering
no civilized god would allow—good souls to bad gods. In silence, in deep
soil, I can hear the shouting—*quando, come, perchè, dove.*

---

quando, come, perchè, dove: when, how, why, where

Dove

Don't we always seem to want to know that life
exists in places other than here? And here, *proprio*,

where the Cortonese may have walled up their doors
of the dead, but still burn kilowatts all night in

the *camposanto*, little lights on graves, while on hot
evenings the living sit on their dark steps in near-shadow.

Where did life begin, where does it? Here Descartes says *penso
dunque sono*, and it's that Latin-like *dunque* dunking

that sentence, the big *therefore*, reminding us there's cause,
therefore effect. And from the thick strings of sperm

unraveling: birth, such as two years ago, such life began in
Poland, Agnieszka begat Maddalena by Jacek, son-in-law

---

dove: where
proprio: right here
camposanto: cemetery
penso dunque sono: I think, therefore I am

of Stanislaw, Polish stonemason in Cortona. He's shown
us pictures of this *bambina*, naked, her pudendum as big

as my fist. *Dunque.* The black-bordered death notices
on the walls of this city—we want to soak our hearts

in their streams of words, leach out any poisons, hate, misery,
fear, greed, anything that takes us away from our own lives

living, our obituaries in some kind of perpetual orbit around
us. *Dunque: dolce far niente*—it is sweet to do nothing. Nothing

from nothing comes nothing. During the day, the lights are off
in the walled *camposanto*. Someone has planted lavender on a new

mound and someone will pick it and hang bundles in dark
closets. *La vita su Marte* is the headline in the *Corriere della*

Sera today, life on the red planet named for the god of war. Seeds
that have floated through space are gathered and crushed in a mortar.

Nascere, crescere—what's happening to the twelve *carciofi* seeds
Bettarelli planted in small clay pots—we give them water each day,

---

la vita su marte: life on Mars
nascere, crescere: to be born, to grow
carciofi: artichokes

a little sun, they send up small leaves. *Dunque* is such a heavy
and final word, unlike the earth we walk upon, turned soil now leveled,

and even softer *erba*, what we lie upon and under, what we cut
and water. We gather seeds. We sow seeds by hand for this greening *erba*.

---

erba: grass

Erbaccia

Especially overwhelmed by weeds
was Walt Whitman. But not grass,
which means *to grow*—it follows

its root word to the letter. And *all flesh
is grass*, St. Somebody said in chapter
something, verse something, in such

and such a book. On my desk, *Foglie
d'erba* has a green cover: "A child
said *What is the grass?* fetching it

to me with full hands." Perhaps
he thought the land the greatest
poem, and that we absorb it through

grass, through wheat, rice, corn,
oats, barley, and rye.
What did Nebuchadnezzar

---

erbaccia: weed
foglie d'erba: leaves of grass

think to himself, on all fours,
naked, eating grass, after all that
power, after all that illusion? Blake

drew him with claws, turning back
into beast, Blake who sat naked
in the tree in his backyard, reading

Milton aloud to his naked wife.
Whitman believed grass was
"the journey-work of the stars."

Driving back from Pienza I saw plows
working under moonlight. What
do we make with one life, a life

watered or a life unwatered, depending
on our needs, our luck, our
time of harvest. I've wanted

the experience of being thoroughly
thrashed on the threshing floor. Or
to be a weed but not weeded,

something growing where it's not
wanted, where the garden pushes
up better things. Bettarelli turns

the ground by hand so the roots
of weeds will die, so the seeds
of weeds won't self-sow. We'd

just as soon forget all the bad things
that have happened in our lives,
instead of turning them over and over,

thinking we'll see a side we haven't
seen, and then, only then there would be grass
growing green. Now we sink the iron *pergola*

into the ground, plant roses and grapes
and jasmine to climb over it—some
things grow where we want them

to grow, take shape, are sometimes
pounded into shape by battered,
black hands of the father, of the *fabbro*.

---

pergola: arbor
fabbro: blacksmith, maker

*F*abbro

Fortunately, I remembered to unplug the espresso machine before the first summer storm hit because I remembered last summer's il tuono, il fulmine. We needed a rod on the roof to catch lines of bright light that happened near us, and when Mario pounded the four-foot-long brass rod into the ground to ground the house, I was relieved. I can't think all day about the gods, or even just good gods, for how little time would be left to think about the bad. Bad meaning bad meaning evil, or even quasi-evil, which is still evil. I could provide you with a list, in case you've forgotten. Let's have a picnic, and if that's too innocent for you, bring your own storms. Già fatto? In a world of emptiness, we'll just have to make do. Uncle Florenty worked at the lumber yard, sawdust in his packs of cigarettes. Make a statement against despair. The issue is time, time, time. Aunt Evelyn cleaned hospital rooms after everyone had died, or just simply had gone home, put one foot in front of the other foot. Uncle Syl loaded boxcars and Uncle Syl unloaded boxcars. Uncle Jack and Aunt Loretta were janitors where I went to college. Make do. Aunt Bernice sold cosmetics and then died earlier than any of the others. I thought it was the factory life for me, living the big lonely fabrication. Storms stir up dust. In the Cortona camposanto, I saw bright clear photographs of Aldo, town hunchback, who

---

fabbro: blacksmith
il tuono, il fulmine: thunder, lightning
già fatto: already done

froze to death a year ago last January, and Roberto, town painter, but quite nuts, too, who wandered with his canvases from *caffè* to *caffè*, late into the night. They are as inert as the silver nitrate that keeps them staring at me. As are all of the above, not *io*, all of them taking turns reading silently their own versions of Dante. *Già fatto*. One prayer: in the gloom of the *fabbro's* house, where on his forge he pounds and pounds, when he takes my tools, *ascia, falce, ronca,* and *zappa*, and straightens them again so I can do what I do, make what I make, see what I see, live what I live—continually, *senza sosta*, a kind of immortality, *una gioia fugace*, an endless day.

---

io: I, me
ascia, falce, ronca, zappa: ax, sickle, pruning hook, hoe
senza sosta: without stopping
una gioia fugace: short-lived joy

Giorni

Gather the pears of St. Peter before the first *vespa* begins to suck
out the white juice, and gather the *nocciole* on St. Philibert's day,

hence their other name, before something I can't see bores small
holes into the brown shells. The long cords of the families continue to

unravel, on one end a weight down an old well, green snakes at the
    bottom.
Gather cabbages when their outer leaves are large enough to wrap

a child in, or when one leaf can be floated in a bucket of water with a
    honey
jar on top. The recipes get longer when I want them shorter, shorter when

I want them longer. The moon is waxing and now what should I be
    gathering?
Gather the *pomodori, sempre*. Snap them off their thick green stems and eat,

---

giorni: days
vespa: wasp
nocciole: hazelnuts
pomodori, sempre: tomatoes, always

the heat of them in your hands. Make a fist of your hand, make a hand of
    your
fist. What's the first stop after death, or the next stop? I remember the years

I spent, cumulatively, below zero, frozen families. Then thawed families,
    gathering
for some reason, and then leaving, saying *tanti auguri*, and may there be one

hundred of these days. The sun gathers the darkness somehow because
    each
day here I sense two minutes less of light. Exactly two, as if someone holds

up two fingers and someone else in the control room nods. Gather the
    melone,
small and sweet, hundreds of seeds in the wet center. Think of the seeds

the families have sown, have scattered. It has been all of us here who have
gathered, even casually, such as, I gather that you're in a hurry, I gather
    that

this is the last time we'll see each other alive. It is I, talking, speaking
    correctly,
writing one last word followed by another last word. I somehow need to

---

tanti auguri: best wishes

gather darkness around me like the shield I want to be carried home on.
When we gather, we recognize what we've gathered. And all the days,

more than the one hundred, more than the thirty thousand we've been
    allotted,
all these days repeat *this is us, it is you, here, it is I, here, sono io.*

---

sono io: it is I

Io

I'm sincere about this:
I think I can smell time:
a needle pushing through
sailcloth in a dark room,
pulling invisible thread.
The field mice who have
taken over the house
no one goes into any longer.
Writing *where* with your finger
in the wet sand. Pulling up
weeds around your father's
grave. Forging some pact
with each day to call it good.
This *Io* isn't the girl Zeus
changed into a white cow,
the one Hera had gadflies
drive into Egypt. This is more
of an *io* like an ion, the time
it takes for the light

---

io: I, me

from the nearly full moon
to pass over this page,
if someone had opened
to this page, if this page
were near a window.
We all know the improbabilities
and yet we all are willing
to live with them. I can't
even dream time away—it's there,
some long rectangular mirror
hidden under the bed.
Today I planted *timo*
outside the kitchen door
to urge spring to come quickly,
even though it's now only the end
of August and I'm leaving here soon.
I'll leave leaves to do their work
of decay without me making
diagrams in the dust of their falling.
It's enough that *timo* will flower
in April with the irises
I'll harvest for their bulbs
before the *istrici* eat them.
If the long days darken,
it won't always be so.

---

timo: thyme
istrici: porcupines

My father worked out
his own life somehow—
everyone has. That's time
there, Beppe bringing thirty
fresh-cut chestnut poles
to use to stake the new olives
that won't bear fruit for years.
He'll ask me to help him,
and together, *insieme*,
we will work.

Lavoro

Let's have a look-see, my father would say to me
when he saw a garage sale sign on someone's lawn,
the two of us nearly scraping the slushy Minnesota
streets in his rusted-out 1949 Dodge. This is 1970
or later or earlier and I feel I'm beginning to learn

to read at eighteen and sit here next to a man of sixty
who still doesn't know how. Today I went down
to the machine shop, to buy *olio* for my *motosega*
and to escape the sixteen thumps per minute
of the new well being pounded into the ground

at the neighbor's house right below—nearly sixty meters
and no water, eight days of pounding earth. And there
among the tractors lined up to be fixed was a *quaranta denti*,
a harrow, and I thought of the harrowing of hell,
such hard labor, but Jesus never seemed to be one

---

lavoro: work
motosega: chain saw
quaranta denti: literally, "forty teeth," a harrow

not to kick the living shit out of a few devils. Harrow also means
to rob, to steal, that he stole the good souls out of hell
(when hell was other people) after his own death.
Lavorare stanca, Cesare Pavese would say. But I can also
see Jesus in blue overalls, riding high on his Pasquali,

whipping that harrow around the devil's lettuces,
like Rome after the Punic Wars ploughing up Carthage,
then harrowing it, then salting the fields. It's harrowing
enough to be alive, without death scaring
the bejesus out of us. We know Flannery O'Connor said that

you don't need Jesus if you've got a good car, but
I'd like to know what kind, make, color, how fast, four- or two-
door, air, back seat big enough to make love, St. Christopher
medals swinging from the mirror and a great good god under
the hood, some god to save us, arising powerfully from this machine.

Lavorare stanca: Working makes you tired

Macchina

My sweat will never be holy enough for angels
to collect in gold cups for some future reliquary.
I work inside in my *stanza di lavoro* or
outside in the *campo*.

                    My fields are poetry and olives.
The two machines I use: one made out of words,
the other mainly metal, fueled by *miscela*,
a *decespuliatore* that can cut the here out of there.

Sweat stains my gloves, makes my boots shine, and
even the horseflies from Placido's two white horses
across the road slide off me.
                        This morning when
I took in the car—simply *una macchina* here—
to find out why it stalled at times, I looked up *stall*
to be able to say *imballare*, the opposite of *ballare*, to dance,
and I thought of the year before my father died,

---

macchina: machine, car
stanza di lavoro: workroom, study
campo: field
miscela: mixture of oil and gasoline
decespuliatore: weed-cutting machine

already he had begun to stall, as his mother did
before she died: and also both danced at odd times,
for no reason, to no music anyone else could hear,
and then they stopped, their engines seized.

La macchina umana, the human body, huffing
and puffing to pull itself through doorways, out
exits, and then gone, truly gone, and in that way

unfixable, unlike the machine below me pounding
a rod into the ground to find water. I heard something
break, and then heard silence and swearing (*porca madonna, ecc.*),
then hammering, then the machine pounding again.

                                                             It wasn't
my father knocking on the door, asking me to help him
clean the barroom he and I cleaned together for ten years,
every Sunday morning at five, asking me to stare with him

out the window, asking me my name, asking me to read him
the poems I've written about him so he could remember
something he forgot, asking me to tell him something

---

porca madonna: literally, "pig mother"

he doesn't know, or does, something greasy and clanky, something that has moving parts, something shiny with bright white fenders, something rolling his way, something immortal, something beautiful, something new.

Notizia

1

Niente di nuovo sotto il sole
and go tell that to someone like Newton,
who, a couple of years past twenty,
that's two zero,
knew all there was to know about light.

2

Science only goes so far—
                                      it takes poets
to imagine the colors contained in white.

3

You want news?
I'll give you news.
This morning I saw Lucifer,

---

notizia: news
niente di nuovo sotto il sole: nothing new under the sun

now called Venus, but I like the old name, too.
Isn't that the word for *match* in Dutch?
For falling bodies, also
see Newton, above.

4

No news isn't really that bad.
But here's a headline: politician kills mother, wife,
advisors, burns the capital. Yes, that's
Nero, last of the Caesars,
all this done before he was thirty,
and those advisors above
were none other than Seneca and Lucan.
Nero actually killed them
by forcing them
to kill themselves.
Surely the top story in the *Acta diurna*,
the first daily newspaper, founded by J. Caesar.

5

Then Nero does himself in and leaves this note:
"What a great artist the world is losing in me."

---

acta diurna: daily acts

6

Ah, *la vita di un poeta*:
all of us trying for the right headline:
someone dies, someone's born:
the great cancellation.

7

            After a time, the great
don't get any better, and then there are those
such as Keats, who wasn't any good while alive,
the newspapers and journals said, but great
after having died.

8

            The headline here
nearly two thousand years after Nero
supposedly crucified St. Peter upside down
(were any crosses made of olive wood?):
the freeze killed so many olive trees,
some so old Hannibal's lone elephant,
marching near Cortona toward Lake Trasimeno,
could have crushed their fruit.
                        One doesn't

---

la vita di un poeta: the life of a poet

have to be twenty-two and Newton to know
falling bodies when one sees falling bodies.
In early December in these fields,
bound by their own laws:
they can be picked by poets and emperors,
shaken from their trees into wide nets,
thousands and thousands of olives.

Oliveto

O
live, dammit, as if your life
depended on it,
I keep telling you.
You've known those misers of life,
who give to no one the nothing
they don't have. *Porca miseria!*
Okay, perhaps I'm being
too harsh, perhaps we should drop
this argument down a notch
or two, but with enough
good strong rope left
to hang yourself from one
of those beautiful olives,
perhaps, to go swinging toward death
with the wind
knocking olive-laden branches
against your body. Again,
forgive the morbidity.
Perhaps it's those Italian newspapers

---

oliveto: olive grove
porca miseria: literally, "pig misery," this miserable life

I've been reading to work on my Italian,
but the articles go into such detail
on killings—as if they still meant
something, an American cynic told me.
Milton said, "An olive leaf he brings,
pacific sign." A little peace
in our time. There are trees
in these fields cut down in 1985
(but reborn), their trunks so large
I could bathe in them.
Uninterrupted life,
unspoiled by unnatural movement,
just a thrush's wing,
just the owl on the windowsill,
just a ladder trapped in a tree,
being set loose by a pair of small hands.
I simply strap a willow basket
around my waist and pick
well after my hands turn green.
Each olive is one-fourth oil
and from hundreds of kilos
we receive hundreds of liters.
It has always been difficult to imagine
anyone betraying anyone else
under the olive trees, as Judas did Jesus,
for example, and then hanged himself
from a branch afterwards. At lunch,
Ben said that the Italian papers

call young boys who kill, *baby-killers*,
words borrowed from English
to name the unnameable. Betray life.
Kill someone for nothing, for nothing.
No thing. No thing. We are all sorry, sorry,
sorry, sorry, sorry, apologetic, yes,
and maimed, full of blame. What
happened or did it not exist (*a land*)
and where (*of wheat and barley*)
who owned it (*and vines and fig trees*)
should we not have taken
that last detour (*and pomegranates*)
those we love to see in December,
split open on their trees (*a land of olive oil and honey*)
thudding to the ground (*root hog or die*)

*P*orca Miseria

Pig!
By that I mean a young hog,
as my hog-loving friends correct me,
or even better, swine,

so easy to recognize if one is able
to cast pearls before them.
They will look out of their pig eyes
quizzically: what the hell is this dude

doing casting pearls? If we have pig misery,
do we have also horse honesty,
cow humility, dog generosity, cat piety?
In our wretched lives, holy hog,

we could console each other with good slop,
converse in *igpay atinlay allay ayday*.
Even though the Germans below me
today have found water at seventy-five meters,

---

porca miseria: literally, "pig misery"

wasser to wash down those sausages
they're fond of, or blood pudding
from St. Pig, I'm not anymore at ease,
even though the well-drilling will soon stop,

but it's that vein of cold water they've struck.
It's too close to the vein of gold
I visit in this chair in this room,
a room that Sig. Cacini,

now dead, lived in when he farmed this land
for the *padrone* who lived in the other part
of the house. The grapes for *vin santo*
hung from wires tied to these chestnut beams.

Pig of summer, hog of fire, sweet swine.
Descendent of the *cinghiale*,
domesticated years before Homer
would have Circe change Odysseus's men

into swine. Alastair found two baby boars
drowned in a shallow well,
perhaps part of the family
that had been eating Rupert's *pomodori*.

---

padrone: owner of the house
vin santo: literally, "holy wine"
cinghiale: wild boar
pomodori: tomatoes

My father, for his family on the farm,
each year butchered
a whole hog. He talked about headcheese
into his eighties. *Questa porca vita.*

That's what Ovid was thinking
the last ten years of his life,
writing letters and poems
back to his friends in Rome,

as he sat in exile
in some fishing village
on the Black Sea. *Vieni qua,*
he would call

across the beach to his dog.
He shouted to his dog
exactly what he himself wanted
to hear: *vieni qua,* Ovid, *vieni qua.*

---

questa porca vita: literally, "this pig life"
vieni qua: come here

Qua

Quaggiù: in this world, in this life.
The point the needle makes

isn't quite enough to see through,
to see over there, là.

These were the words we used
the summer of 1991, qui/qua—

here where we are.
Li/là—there where we will be.

The four Polish men who helped us
clear fields taught us their tu/tam,

Pick up this rock tu
and move it tam.

These tanned working bodies of ours,
children of Sisyphus, moved half a world

---
quaggiù: in this world
qua: here

in this life, hither and thither,
il mondo di qua, this world.

If out of the quarrel with time
we make tracks, and if out of

the quarrel with fate, we make bets,
or if out of the quarrel with Italians,

we make pasta, or if out of the quarrel
with God, we make believe,

and if out of the quarrel
with our bodies, we make love,

then qui per qui, here's the here
and now. We go as far as the quadrivio

and, like Robert Johnson, we fall down
on our knees. Quid pro quo.

Believe in the here because
there's no there there, or believe

in the there because there's no
here here. Would I translate hereafter

---

qui per qui: here and now
quadrivio: crossroads

as *quadopo*? Out of the quarrel
with love, we make out, make waves.

One can have passion only
for the moment, and the moment

passes. But then we go,
we catch up, and then more passion.

Out of the quarrel
with the here, we've made there.

Perhaps. But out of the quarrel
with the sun, the sun here

and now, we've made hay,
we've brought in, we've gathered

everything alive at the moment,
becoming part of the great good harvest.

Raccolta

Read them and weep,
my college poker buddies
loved to say. Then
two hands
would gather
pennies, nickels,
and dimes. We who
sometimes played
together until sunrise
have all left the table,
pack of worn blue cards
unshuffled. Every night
the old men of Torreone
play, outside, in front
of the *caffè*, all *pensionati*,
slapping cards on the plastic
tables. *Contadini*, nearly all
of them, when they walk
by my house know

---

raccolta: harvest, gathering
pensionati: retired people
contadini: farmers

where wild lettuces grow
on the roadside, pop them out
with their penknives.
Some put in a small crop
of *granturco* to feed the geese
and chickens. Read them
and weep—I'd slip
and say *reap*—same idea.
"Your descendants shall gather
your fruits," Virgil said
in the *Eclogues*:
Carpent tua poma nepotes,
and I have the picture
of Adam scything wheat
in his t-shirt, Eve gathering
the stems in bundles.
Then after we've gathered,
what? Stand in the aftermath,
hands in pants pockets,
will there be the moon
opening up, remnants
of its light hiding in this same field
in December, light snow
in what were furrows?
No one wept.

---

granturco: literally, "Turkish grain"; American corn

The olives give up their olives,
but keep their leaves.
It's September—soon grape knives
and scissors will be sharpened
for the *vendemmia*,
a cool red cluster,
a cool gold *grappolo*,
filling up the red buckets
—our stand against
the short life. In December
what we've gathered
will be ready: wine flows
into terra cotta pitchers,
on all the tables,
wine black or white,
brimming in the clear glasses,
loose, *sfuso*,
its taste taking us
where it wants us to go.

---

vendemmia: harvest
grappolo: a bunch of grapes
sfuso: loose, unpackaged

Sfuso

Smell that!
Can you smell
that? Sunday 10 A.M.,
under any
window in Cortona.
First food. The white
clank of plates, *ragù, pane,
odori*, through the closed
shutters. The rabbits
in the *macelleria*—some
fur is left on to
remind you you're not
buying cat. There are
many of those, tough,
half-skinned from fights
over *topini*. I caught
one of the latter in
the cantina and set

---

ragù, pane, odori: pasta sauce, bread, a vegetable base for sauces
macelleria: butcher's shop
topini: small mice

it loose in the *camposanto*
so it could make
nests in the hair
of the just-dead. Across
the road, Placido
keeps his falcon in a grand
cage. We see it tear
into a live quail
during its exercise
run. Loosen
the chains, loosen
the chains!
I wish the world
were shouting all
together. Poetry
is *un linguaggio
scuro*. My father
pulled the plug
on his mother and
we pulled
the plug on him,
freed him
from death. What
must one do to loosen,

---

un *linguaggio scaro*: an obscure language

to unhitch, to open
so that which rises
can go up?
Freedom may just
be a come-on. Loosen
the control that light has
over light. Shine a little
darkness on the subject. Loosen
the soil where we'll plant *carciofi* in October,
aglio in December, aster
and chrysanthemums—
flowers for the grave,
flowers coming back out of the ground.

---

aglio: garlic

Terreno

This *terraferma*—that much I know.
        Quarantacinque anni fa
I wasn't yet born,
        couldn't yet die. Forgive me
but I'm a little confused about time.
        I do remember
when my parents canceled our subscription
        to *Life*—too much
of it bourgeois for the proto-Marxists
        that they were.
I want to be confronted with the fact
        of the future. Dig a hole
and fill it with the past,
        and dig a long trench
and fill it with the present.
        What will grow from either?
I want to hide among the weeds
        the soil pushes up and out,
become the weed I have become. I've often bought

---

terreno: land, ground, subject matter
terraferma: dry land
quarantacinque anni fa: forty-five years ago

        a five-subject
notebook, thinking . . . . It *seems* right,
        five subjects,
that's all there are. In the taxi today
        in Firenze,
the light changed
        and it was suddenly fall. To be
any more worldly than I am,
        I'd have to eat dirt.
When I get to the end
        of this poem,
you will know it—there's a low stone wall
        there, four
or five vines sinking under the weight
        of their grapes.
Beyond that I don't go.
        The light changed,
we went through the intersection,
        it started raining.
I bought white grapes from Puglia
        and washed them
in the hotel sink.
        Move the fences
but the land stays put. While hoeing around vines,
        I cut
a green snake in two,
        its then helpless tail thrashed
for ten minutes,

trying to will itself back
on the rest of the body.
What would it be like
to be otherworldly, coughing on the red gases
of Jupiter's
moons, paddling a canoe
in the canals of Mars.
Whoever said I wasn't down
to earth, sometimes waist deep
in some *fossa*
I'm digging,
that's the recipe for strong stems,
the dark bunches hanging
upon them,
so simple, good,
true, not exactly our opposites,
no, but what have we learned?
Love,
is that the right news to bring
to this hill, rampant
with vine and grape?

---

fossa: ditch, pit

Uva

You, Virgil,
        day breaks for you
                as for us,
and night falls
        for you, Virgil, as for
                us. Although
my parents
        didn't read aloud to me
                your poems,
neither in your
        Latin nor their English,
                I watched them
act out your *Georgics*,
        even act out those lines
                you discarded, deleted,
scratched out
        with a goose feather, lines
                any of us would

---

uva: grape
Georgics: from the root word for farming

    trade our houses
               and cars for. If Keats had lived,
                             would he have lived
in your Rome, riding
            his little horse from there to Mantua,
                        to your farm,
sitting in your olive
            groves, breathing English air
                          into Aeneas? Would he
have written his
            name in oil? Truth, beauty,
                        beauty, truth,
the mantra on my screen
            saver, scrolls across the monitor
                        even when I'm not
there to notice. Today
            I strolled past Dante's house
                        and Dante's church,
where he would see
            Beatrice and invent noncorporeal
                        love for a real woman,
dead not much later
            in the Plague. You, Virgil, didn't walk
                        through the paradise
of that world—this Roman
            one of yours was enough. If Aeneas
                        found Rome and you
found Aeneas and

    then Keats found Rome, after traveling
          days in a carriage from Naples,
and then she found and he
    found and they found and we found and I
        found . . . . Roman stone
to walk upon as you left
    the millions of Roman ghosts who have
        lived here and are now walking
in other kinds of paradise.
    That is, Virgil, when the entire *vigna* is
        down to one grape, *un chicco*
d'uva, you are standing,
    watching it drop into the dirt—this
        too is *la Venere*, this too is *la verità*.

---

vigna: vineyard
un chicco d'uva: one grape
la Venere: beauty
la verità: truth

Verità

Vincerò, sings
Jussi Bjorling,
Puccini's *Turandot*
crackling on 78
turned into CD.
These are the late
'90s. That was
the late '30s.
He had better
lungs than God.
Verily I say unto
you that it is easier
to listen to *Turandot*
than to have composed
it. Truth is farther
than one can see,
more than one
can hear. If Keats
took truth to his

---

verità: truth
vincerò: I will win

grave, he was
a beautiful corpse.
Gimme body
any day. I say it
as a hedge
against mortality.
All of those
gathering for
the *vendemmia*,
cutting a few
pounds of truth
from the vines,
with one beautiful
stroke of the knife.
Whenever I'm feeling
overly spiritual, I fly
around this room
for a while, then
become self-conscious,
and crash into
the furniture. Earth
is truth, too.
What we walk upon,
what we go down
into. Stevens said that the world's

---

vendemmia: harvest

ugly, that everyone on it
is sad. If what we
touch touches us
back, if what we hear
hears us back, if
what we taste
tastes us back,
if what we smell
smells us back, if what
we see sees us back.
Isn't *Inferno* better
than *Paradiso*? Isn't it
that when we write
happiness we mean
beauty? Puccini writes
it, Jussi sings it,
we hear it, coming
out the double doors
into the front yard,
mixing with the jasmine
and geraniums,
the hyssop,
the stŭ-ōne
of the stone walls,
I will win, he sings,
whether it's beauty
or truth, who knows,
and has he won

already, past tense,
since that's all he
knows on earth,
this earth upon which
we will soon gather
for the olive harvest,
when not long ago white
oxen snorted in the cold
fields, for spring had
called, and said it would
soon return, to turn
the soil, the earth,
the truth, turn it with plow
and shovel, *aratro* and *vanga*,
find the beauty
that will come,
prepare for it,
use well the hoe,
the *zappa*, get down
on your knees and dig.

---

aratro: plow
vanga: shovel
zappa: hoe

Zappa

Zeno, nearly blind, needed to walk
across his kitchen to see time

on the wall clock but could only make it
to the middle, and then only the middle

of the middle of the middle of the middle.
Tempus fugit, or, in other words,

"we was robbed." A little *zucchero*
in my endless thimbleful of espresso

to help jump start what stalls, such as
time stalling, zapping the zeros off

the centuries until all I find myself
with is a *zolla*, a little bit of land,

---

zucchero: sugar
zappa: hoe

and a hoe in my two hands.
Will the ground forgive the blade the dullness

the blacksmith will soon grind away?
How much truth is there in one grape,

or grapes gathered in tight bunches on vines?
They're backlit with today's news

that Zephyrus blows in, big Botticelli breath
blowing Venus across water: love's movement

toward love. After World War II, Zappini
walked home from Russia to see time

on his unborn son's face. Both men have helped
me make these fields be fields. We grind

our edges to make them true, grind away
the history of stony soil. "To cut one's

throat" is *darsi la zappa sui piedi*,
but the hoe won't reach the foot, only goes

---

darsi la zappa sui piedi: literally, "to cut one's feet with a hoe"

halfway to it, and halfway to that halfway mark.
Horses stand in their stalls, in love

with their stasis, memories of manes in wind.
The west wind blows darkness toward lightness

or away from even more darkness. The light's red:
no one appears to be moving. In the museum,

I go around and around the painted vases,
youth wrestling lion, chariot pulled by horses,

young girl about to say something no one
has said before. And then the ground breaks

open by an olive or chestnut or
pomegranate, yes pomegranate, so small

we can't yet see it. Should we break
the needle after mending something so

the something stays mended? Zeros fall
on the ground. The hoe leans

against the cherry tree. This was time
used to break apart time

to make more time happen
  in time to come, and to give time

  to what had happened
  what seems like a long time ago.

Cortona and San Francisco
August–September, 1996

Acknowledgments

My appreciation to the editors of the following journals in which poems from this book, some in earlier versions, were first published: *Colorado Review* ("Verità"); *Epoch* ("Erbaccia," "Fabbro," and "Io"); *Gettysburg Review* ("Dove"); *Indiana Review* ("Buii"); *Southern Review* ("Ago" and "Campo"); and *Southwest Review* ("Giorni").

Thanks to Santa Clara University for a sabbatical, and to the National Endowment for the Arts for a Poetry Fellowship. Many thanks to Josephine Carson; Serena Caressi; Francesco and Giorgio Zappini; Giuseppe Agnolucci; Riccardo Bertocci and Amy Lumpkin; Rupert and Donatella Palmer; Placido, Fiorella, and Chiara Cardinali.